RIPPER!

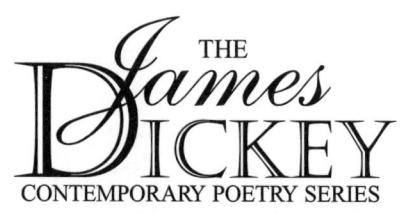

THE
James
DICKEY
CONTEMPORARY POETRY SERIES

EDITED BY RICHARD HOWARD

RIPPER!

Carl Jay Buchanan

UNIVERSITY OF SOUTH CAROLINA PRESS

Published in Columbia, South Carolina, by the
University of South Carolina Press

Manufactured in the United States of America

03 02 01 00 99   5 4 3 2 1

Library of Congress Cataloging-in-Publication Data

Buchanan, Carl Jay, 1961–
    Ripper / Carl Jay Buchanan.
        p.   cm.

    ISBN 1-57003-297-1 (alk. paper)
    ISBN 1-57003-298-X (pbk. : alk. paper)
    1. Jack, the Ripper—Poetry.   2. Whitechapel (London, England)—
History—Poetry.   3. Serial murders—England—London—History—
19th century—Poetry.   I. Title.
PS3552.U319 R57   1999
811'.54—dc21   98-58088

The author offers grateful acknowledgment to the editors of the follow-
ing publications, in which some of the material in this book originally
appeared, sometimes in slightly different form: *Paris Review,* "Victims";
Chicago Review, "The Prince"; *Kansas Quarterly,* "Jacks to Open"; and
Louisville Review, "Hide 'n' Seek."

Publication of this book was supported by a grant from the Eric Matthieu
King Fund of The Academy of American Poets.

For Kristine, Miranda, and Corey
and in memory of Savannah

I am a man; I count nothing human foreign to me.

—Terence

But principally I hate and detest that animal called man . . .

—Swift

Contents

A Note on Carl Buchanan and *Ripper!*

"I began writing it fourteen years ago"—a letter from the poet acknowledges as long ago as 1994; and his book is as intricately formed as that long gestation would suggest (compel), a series of structures within structures, like those Chinese boxes which sanction entrance—and egress—through an invisible sliding panel, itself to be discovered only by a process of trial and error (what a phrase for this subject!); and once inside the innermost (and empty!) chamber, nowhere to go but out again, the Gentle Reader's tormented spirit seeking release as it had first sought enthralment.

This systole and diastole, a dialectic of confinement and compurgation that makes for the doubleness of all rhythm, is wonderfully observed in *Ripper!,* a text which for merely *narrative* purposes would otherwise confound the reader. I mean that given the nature of what is being returned to and issued from, any regular compositional procedures among those which we associate with verse, any ceremonial of recurrence, would afford us a kind of discouragement, a hypnosis of horror.

After all, the poet has chosen to assemble his great inquiry—what is the self? how is an individual to be identified, who am I?—around the most sensational (and unsolved) serial-murder case in modern history, and he has been unsparing in the freshness and frequency of the details. Only by ringing changes in his formal enterprise, by keeping the reader guessing (and hoping that the guesses are *wrong*), can Carl Buchanan be certain that we do not go the way of all crime buffs, all enthusiasts of detection who abandon their text once the solution is achieved, to the point of forgetting the phraseology itself. Here of course, as in all poetry, it is *the phraseology itself* which is at issue, and at closure, and Buchanan has ensured the avoidance of any monotony, any favor of forgetting, by an interlocking configuration of poems of the most iridescent variety; indeed *Ripper!* is actually what the classical rhetoricians call Menippean satire, wherein debate and disguise replace any (mere) linear occasion.

The *frisson* afforded by a celebrated (public) criminal instance has been of great appeal to writers in our developing media culture—from Dostoievsky down to Don DeLillo, and from Thom Gunn (songs for Jeffrey Dahmer, no less) back to Robert Browning, whose discovery of the "square old yellow book," a baroque Roman murder story, was to generate one of the two greatest nineteenth-century English epics of murder and adultery (the other is *The Idylls of the King*). Yet even so virtuosic a manipulator of blank verse as Browning collides with the problem of formal *longueurs:* why should every member of his (extremely varied) personnel employ the same prosodic structure? Here is where Carl Buchanan has discerned and seized a great advantage: conscious that today's readers are by no means so ready to invest in extended iambic-pentameter discourse as Browning's more acquiescent public (by the time he was writing *The Ring and The Book,* Browning actually had a public), Buchanan has sought, and with the permission of our incomparable modernity has found, the most sensitive variations within free-verse utterance, where finding must mean *invention,* that chief virtue of the grand poem, as is asserted, once again, by the classical rhetoricians.

Inevitable bewilderment is a part of this learned maker's stratagem—it is only when the whole poem has closed over us that we know where we are, and where we want to be: at the heart of the mystery disclosed *as mystery,* not dismissed as solution. We stick with the poem, or rather it sticks with us, because it is not resolved, not settled, not *known.* It is a difficult, very modern beauty which is the consequence of Carl Buchanan's architecture and interior design; *Ripper!* is like one of those disquieting new buildings—examples in Tokyo, in Bilbao, in Mexico City—in which and from which we may learn to renegotiate space, to reconceive desire, to redefine the self.

Richard Howard

RIPPER!

Introduction to the Ripper

For months the night stalker
moved through alleys of filth
in London's shadowed corner,
choosing his victims at seeming
random (although the pattern of deaths
shapes a cross on the East End map).
At least six, perhaps twenty-seven
whores or mere sluts he disembowelled,
stabbed to sieves, de-breasted, placing
both slices on eyeballs, or just ripped.
The papers and prudish Victorian crowds
named him gentleman, butcher, ex-sailor,
or zealous reformer calling the eyes of the Mass
to the horrible conditions of the poor
in the greatest city in the world
(he may have been quite religious).
They dubbed him Jack (like John Doe,
an unknown everyman). He sent some letters
to the papers, to officials, and once
a piece of human kidney to the Whitechapel Vigilance
Committee. I think he liked Poe; both were
haunted carvers of the soul, each had
damned strange ideas about women.
Bobbies (Peelers) wore dresses, some say,
to lure him out of the famous yellow
fogs—they stood on every half-block,
and still he killed. No one
ever claimed the rewards, but on a good
note, reform to Whitechapel, new laws for
the slums finally came. Of course you know
the killings just stopped, and he never was
caught. He's the best known, more important
and mysterious serial killer, the sickest
avatar of Conscience.

Jacks to Open

Jack to Emma Smith
3 April 1888 London

The first time I cut off a whore's ear
I didn't understand. I thought it was revenge
for my reflection, but I saw nothing
later, in shop windows at fake dawn,
except shoddy displays anyone with a soot
smudge of talent might draw. I am an artist
perhaps; I'm sure she understood behind the mask
of a face needing one good rip. She was ripped,
say drunk—she kept calling to others, though
I alone held her arms tight. She spoke to four
of us—one whose forehead and hair glowed
in her painclear sight. Another was pale
and smelled of a livery, held a huge curved
blade not a knife. I was not any of them, I'm sure—
I was first to discover the truth for death's sake,
the student learning glee's flop
in the play of a corpse. And one other
(just before it ended)
she saw had breasts full as lamps in a dark sky,
sharp lies, lips daggers. She cried *Morther!*
or something as I pierced her cunt
and jammed blade to the back. Wanted one hole
foul as the other, sweet as reason. Why
I left her alive, I don't know.

Jack to Martha Tabram, Stabbed 39 Times
7 August 1888 London

Martha once I believed the magic
of numbers. I thought women were spirits
who could not be plumbed by love like an arrow
passing through breasts and out through the upper
triangles where the ripe hand pulls hard, raking
shards of the heart, notched feathers. I lived
with some witches who thought they were different,
felt more, knew the shaping of powers
you and I buried. We sacrificed (goats, cats,
some virgins though how you can tell). One day
they betrayed me—a night I was too shy to mount
in their sight. I knew if I stayed I was next—
one woman's black eyes
watched. Her face held two graves, so I filled
one of them in the spring. There must be one
more, and that's you. With this blade I strike
to be free of the circled pentagram
I could never step out of,
once in. Twice *thirteen for the coven,*
you and me. One more flock of bloodbirds
for her. Say a charm dear it's over
with this.

Jack to Polly Nichols
31 August 1888 London

I too can't stay home. I am driven out nights
by the paving-stones' song, brickmold,
and the gutter's low call. Life's too short
without gin (are you only 42) well your eldest
must be quite the man. Five children? Your ex
stopped the five shillings last week? Here's a bit
for your troubles, I've a bottle and a room
and a long cure near. Hand me back
my bag. No I'm not a doctor. Nor priest,
child. I'm no baby's father—call me lover, 'though
really I'm Bert. The way my dear
in the playhouse doorway crinoline laced
your knee as you paused backlit. Way your fine
shoulders caught at the light, yes
that bone. Let me kiss those lips and these.
Call me anything you like, I'm like you,
I don't care. I'll call you mother, as those
I've watched do. To a cheaper existence
we go, some say better. I'll not go
that far, but one thing I'm sure of
I'll say—
call me Jack.

Jack to Annie Chapman (For Virginia Poe, called Annie
  in his poems)
8 September 1888 London

Poe thought nothing would ever part him
from the nymphet he loved, but the light
in the eyes of his Annie
is out. Neither angels nor demons, when she was Lenore,
understood his views
of Helen in the full moon. Let raven meet
a black cat—say "shadow" four times in the midst
of El Dorado—Ulalume and Tamerlane are ways
of meeting your near self's ghost. Jack to Annie, Jack
and Allan, William Wilson, Edgar Allan to themselves
are doubles, aliens
in silent corners, melancholy as gravesods. Seek the gold
threads of her hair—
but that gay bowl too is broken, wind breaks
the heartsealed shutters, heavy curtains
rustle from the strains of a mad viol
alone. In you, Annie
Chapman of Whitehall, my halfcentury corpse, my
Annabel Lee, for you, Poe, too alone
from childhood's hour, and never never
as others—
your soul *was* a stagnant tide, memory's ruin,
but I love you and love what you loved.

Jack to Cathy and Liz
30 September 1888 London

"The Juwes are not the men that will be blamed
for nothing."—chalked in his hand on a brick wall.

Did I wrestle an angel? *Something* lowered
that night, white forms on its shoulders that throng
like furies' wings in my mind. In the dark I was taken
to a mountain where's hardly a hill. The white rod
broke the red sea. She stood, thighs forward, hands
reaching for me, and I struck but only a woman
fell, red lace on her throat. Between the police
rounds, I was lifted again. Voices hardly made sense—
> white handkerchief with red border
> two short clay pipes
> a blunt table knife, bone handle
> a red mitten and red cigarette case
> with a white metal fitting
her black wrap, imitation fur collar, the dark
skirt I pushed above her thin tits. Then I was struggling
again with God's monster, pushing some devil's throat
into dust. This is nothing.
Don't blame jews. We give our own curses and wrestle
each night in this land of angels like devils like us.

Jack to the Yard
9 November 1888 London

You will not discover in Mary Kelly's retinal impressions,
who.
This theory from fiction that the image last seen at death
is stamped on eyeballs' skin is false—I never see anyone
in my mirror. Sometimes in a chamber of moonlight, I hear bells
inside bells. In the fog no one moves, until eyeball
to nostril contact's shock is swift, gone. She waited
for any John like me on a corner, under a lamp, halo of damp
air. She was not pretty, but beauty's no matter
in the dark, in her room. Impressions should cut
deeper than skin's glimmer or dull cast or pockmarked ravage—
to the guts of the quick.
When I laid her
open and smelled not cheap scent
but the rich gust of blood
swelling out, I knew layers
of gorgeousness her skin
had trapped. When I kissed her heart like a lover
I came,
and no, no wane still when I held her closest
and told her my name, knowing
hers by the yield
of a kidney—truth's vein.

Victims

Emma Smith to Jack the Ripper
3 April 1888 London

Why did his face change
as he struck me with his big knife
like a club? He was a copper, he said,
then became some fop who stuck me and whispered,
"Pig. You delight me, Pig!" As though I haven't heard
and seen and done it, every last low trick. But his features
dripped and fell, flexed into other juts and clefts
till his clay hands worked the blade's tip like a paintbrush.
You know, an artist-chap's. Re-arranged my parts, he did,
as if he tried to see me from four sides at once, and I glimpsed
his inside. Raving but quiet all the same, he was. He called
me Daughter, and I'm damned, but I thought
he did look a tad like the old man,
but then lunatics and leerers look the same, right?
Right? So how then did he put on tits
that sagged like mum's, how did he paint
himself with her own face, and ask me in her voice
if I wouldn't mind
being a good girl, stop
screaming, eat this
now, be good child
or some bogeyman
will come.

Martha Tabram to Jack the Ripper
7 August 1888 London

Sisters, sisters, we all are witches here. Brewing
something that needs bloody water, eyes and soul,
brings us together. Knitting a shroud with a name
in each stitch, a red shawl for eternity
to set off paling bones, keeps us hale,
we moon-wise crones that won't give up our ghosts.
I be only newly dead, but I hold your mirror,
sisters. In the coming months and months
you will be sent by the killer Jack
to mate with me in making the broth
that is perhaps an Excuse
for our stirring chant. Our round-lay, sung in parts,
is our hearts' wail
before the muscle gasps a last fist
and splays—our song, I know, will gain
blood rhythm as your tainted strains join
with mine: you, Annie; you, Elizabeth;
you, Mary; I, Martha; nameless others I can't see
in the cauldron where I pooled my eyes to gain this Sight.
We've a tale to weave, a ballad
of a princess born to an evil king. He slew
her mother and locked the girl in a casket shaped
like the high queen's corpse. He hung the key
at his waist, and visited her, a daily nightmare. The key
shone, a knife of bonelight in the dark side
of the sleeping maid. Come let us tell the song
and quicken candles with unseen breaths in every castle,
for we must cook and stir the dark truth
and the liver, and what else
we can discover, who can See now we be blind.

Polly Nichols to Jack the Ripper
31 August 1888 London

42 years old. I've got five of 'em. My husband used to give
me five shillings, but he's dropped that
since last week, so here I am. Thirsty? Sure,
as much as a codfish. Thanks, kind sir. What's in the bag?
All right, I didn't mean a thing, you're testy,
but you're nice. Haven't I seen you, walking about here
as I do, not really to *do* anyone, if you take
my meaning, but only to walk? The long nights
hold another life, for me. It's the brats
all day, and sometimes I get a lucky customer then too,
and I've got nowhere to go and do a man
but home, and home's just the one room, and the children
stare. So how about here in the alley, this nice lane,
sort of? I lean forward, hike the curtains d'you see, now
you can get in easy, that's it, slide
it in back there, I'm always wet. It's the way
I'm made, like made for love
some gent says to me once. Not my husband,
that shit. Well go ahead and do it love.
I haven't got
all night.
Are you finished
yet?

Annie Chapman to Jack the Ripper
8 September 1888 London

I am not your Annabel Lee. I've read Poe,
or heard him, at least, from my Da
in his cups. He liked to ring the American's bells,
bells, bells, and he swung his rum bottle
about our small room as his voice swelled
and pealed with the flying doomed souls
symbolized, I suppose, by those maddening
bells. He's in Bedlam, that's fact, what was called
Bethlehem once, shortened in name and changed in sense.
Yes even misnamed whores can go *incogito*. That's Latin.
I am who I make me, not men or any woman. I will not fulfill
your ideal, nor recite for you further. I will be one
in Paradise when you lie howling, or you haunt
genteel rooms chained as a damned spirit, doubtless
seeking the virtue you have rent with your crimes.
Curse me, you, you are not
Edgar Allan, bright dome, sunken eyes, cream hands, but I swear
I am the raven who
will sit and peck your eyes out in the night
like mournful and never-ending
Remorse.

Cathy and Liz to Jack the Ripper
30 September 1888 London

Because he paired us, both slain in one night,
we are twins in the Ripper's sky,
a sort of negative Gemini. Our sockets darken
rather than shine. About us is infinite light
but we hook hands and look lost, two dark holes
for our shoulders and two for our breasts,
two for knees, and for feet, two black eyes.
If you see us walking, perhaps as near
as Soho, know what ghosts can do—
lean on each other's lily arm, compare wound-shapes,
swap what we first thought when asking him,
"Care to show a girl a good time?" and whether she
liked his moustache or I his broad build.
God, he was handsome, he who split me
like a fruit, but she or I says, No,
he was a brute like most of them. We argue
out the nights on the Vegas Strip, near Second Street
in Salt Lake City, and sometimes we let
gas light from 1888 shine through our bosoms
as we ask a stranger, a tall one,
"Care to give
a girl a light?"

Mary Kelly to the Yard and Jack the Ripper
9 November 1888 London

You will not discover in my dying body's kidney's yield,
who.
All your theory of that and the other is false. Nor is any
woman simple. We encompass men before they're birthed
and surround them in their manhood and weave
their graveclothes, mourning the rot of what we created.
All men of women born are,
and all women, all mankind. When you locked
the door as I turned my back to raise the gas
in a room my body buys, or bought, and my
not half-bad face, I knew you were one, Jack, a man
who understands in that special way we know ourselves.
We are your betters. Bleeding is
our life's chore. Storing the blood like honey in our cells
for timed release is a mystery
we wrap our legs around and hold
as we lock men's heads
in that worshiping position
as I held yours once, Jack,
before you were born perhaps,
before I named you my son (as I do now)
and out of my Curse came
your head and those blood-filled hands
and the scream of us all,
all, all.

A Note on Ripperology

In writing the awards statement for the KQ/KAC Poetry Awards for 1988/1989, Jonathan Holden noted, "I have a bias toward poems which, instead of recapitulating conventional lyric subject matter—love, death, seasonal changes—have more 'prose'-like subject matter such as history, politics, philosophy. I have a bias toward poems which produce not only a brief shiver and shock of recognition (*Sine qua non!*), but which contain information." In awarding Fourth Prize, which he gave to the first three Ripper poems (considered as one poem), Holden added "[This is] a poem painstakingly researched and rendered in Jack's voice. . . ."

There *is,* in fact, some research supporting these poems, and some historical fact. A Works Consulted would include the six or eight best-known books of Ripperology (a term Colin Wilson, the phenomenologist, coined for Jack the Ripper studies) along with Poe's stories and poems in any edition. My poems also make passing references to Van Gogh's *Letters,* the Old Testament, and an interview I made with a coven of witches in Wichita almost two decades ago. Primarily, however, these poems owe their verisimilitude to the only essential work on the Whitechapel murders, *The Complete Jack the Ripper* by Donald Rumbelow, published in 1987. This study by a City Police officer of London gave me such details as the inset lines of "items found on the deceased" in "Jack to Cathy and Liz." The actual items in her pockets at the time of Catherine Eddowes' death were, according to Rumbelow,

> a white handkerchief with a red border, a match box containing
>   cotton, a blunt
> table knife with a white bone handle, two short clay pipes, a red
>   cigarette case
> with a white metal fitting, a printed handbill, five pieces of soap,
>   a small tin box
> containing tea and sugar, a portion of a part of spectacles, a
>   three-cornered check
> handkerchief, a small comb, a red mitten and a ball of worsted.

That list is found on his page 53; for the poem, I selected these details:

white handkerchief with red border
two short clay pipes
a blunt table knife, bone handle
a red mitten and red cigarette case
   with a white metal fitting.

The facts have been whittled down to their symbolic essentials.

The victims' names, their dates of death, certain details of their murders and of their lives, and other bits are all authenticated by Rumbelow and other researchers. An intriguing example is the handwriting on the wall in "Jack to Cathy and Liz." Although there's much fascinating conjecture about the term "juwes" in Ripperology, I've used it as a variant of Jews, who were still persecuted in nineteenth-century London despite Disraeli's prominence as on-again, off-again Prime Minister. (Gladstone, of course, was "on" when Disraeli was "off.")

The Ripper, whoever he was, was a figure of many personalities, and the variety of methods shown in his crimes indicates to most Ripperologists an unstable sense of self. He may have been any of the various suspects: a minister, doctor, leather-aproned butcher, a student or an artist, the future King Edward VII's eldest son, and so on; new suspects continue to crop up, as in Stephen Knight's 1976 study, *Jack the Ripper: The Final Solution.* This ongoing search is the basis for the identity search in these poems: as the public has wondered for a century, perhaps Jack himself wondered who he was, or who he became when he killed. My poems have this search as a vein of truth helixing through them, from "I am an artist perhaps" to Jack's (imagined?) coven experience, culminating in the last poem's "I never see anyone in mirrors," where the self has evaporated into fog; that's how his search, and mine ends. He's still unknown.

One of the notions original with me is that the pattern of deaths shapes a cross on the East End map. Trace it out.

Was Jack an avid reader of Poe? Perhaps he wanted to *live* Poe's assertion about poetry, that "the death, then, of a beautiful woman

15

is, unquestionably, the most poetical topic in the world" ("The Philosophy of Composition"). All the victims were plain-looking or worse, however; did this feed Jack's rage? In my fourth poem, I allude to several of Poe's well-known verses. As the Ripper kills a prostitute named Annie, he insanely celebrates Poe's dead child-bride Virginia, whom Poe wrote about as "Annie" and "Annabel Lee." In the latter poem concerning necrophilia, the speaker lies down with his wife in her tomb by the sounding sea, which, like the raven, was to Poe "emblematical of Mournful and Never-ending Remembrance." Sleeping with a corpse as a ballad theme is Gothicism of a sort the Ripper would have reveled in; as Poe said, "the truly passionate will comprehend me." (Incidentally, he sets here the tone T. S. Eliot will adopt in *his* best-known essay.)

The witch-Jack of poem the second is not historical, but the thirty-nine stab wounds in Martha Tabram are fact. 39 = 3 x 13, the unlucky number of witches in a coven. I believe this total is not arbitrary, any more than is the coinciding of the numbers of passengers and stab wounds in Agatha Christie's *Murder on the Orient Express*.

Polly Nichols, the third victim, hence subject of the third poem, did have five children and an ex-husband who, at the time of her demise, had just stopped her five-shilling "allowance." (He'd "just stopped" it six years before, at which time she'd turned to prostitution for child support.)

Based on the known and hypothesized "facts," these poems depart from them carefully. So much will always remain obscure about these haunting events; that makes them good dramatic monologue material, I think, since we know too much about Victoria or Gladstone or Oscar Wilde. Their imagined statements in verse would allow much less imagination and less play; so would a Life of an entirely fancied character, who flourished during the same decade. We are too well nourished with Holmesian data, even to the point of knowing where he kept his tobacco (a Persian slipper's toe). We know the pattern exactly of the labyrinth of *his* mind; it's the stories' latent subject.

I can't say for sure whether Jack was black or white. That leaves me with a good deal to *say*.

Suspects: Facts and Theories

Even the number of victims is uncertain. Many murders, some more bizarre or gruesome than others, were committed in that area in those days. Was there what we could call a modus operandi? This is also in dispute. Were they chloroformed to make the murders easier? Did Jack present himself to these streetwalkers as a John? Allow me to introduce some possibilities.

Neill Cream   ONE

In 1892, as Neill Cream was having his neck broken by the hangman's rope, he uttered, "I am Jack the . . . ." Billington, the hangman, swore to this. Known as the Lambeth Poisoner, Cream had poisoned four whores with strychnine, as popular then as it is now. He seems to have been a habitual offender, and was in fact in prison from 1881 to 1891—the Ripper murders occurred while he was securely locked up at Joliet in the U.S.

He may have wanted to be known as Jack for additional notoriety after his death, as though being the Lambeth Poisoner weren't enough fame. But why did he wait till the very last moment to shout "I am Jack the . . . ," not even giving himself time to add "Ripper" very fast (it can be said intelligibly in $1/2$ second by my watch). Also, a Commissioner of Police who was present at Cream's execution never mentioned a last-second cry of any kind in his own autobiography, which he'd surely have done had it occurred, since it makes a great anecdote.

The theory that Cream had a double, and he and his look-alike alternated time in penitentiaries to give each other alibis, is, again, a good story, top-notch fiction. So is the notion that Neill Cream bribed the Chicago Police to let him out early—many documents and witnesses attest that he served his full term.

As a doctor and an abortionist and a skillful poisoner of slatterns, Cream might have become a successful figure of True Horror in his own right, if Jack, being uncaught, did not endlessly tantalize our imaginations with speculations as to his true identity. It's about as certain as that Queen Victoria wasn't a man, that Cream wasn't Jack, and that's sure enough for us. Although in some of the diminutive queen's portraits, there's that moustache shadow . . . .

Dr. Stanley, I Presume   TWO

The widowed "Dr. Stanley" had a son who died early in 1888 as a result of contracting syphilis from a high-class tart, Mary or Marie Kelly. The well-to-do doctor set out with a scalpel, a knife, or a complete set of surgical instruments to avenge his young son's death (actually the son died too soon for his death to have been caused by the ravages of syphilis, a really horrid disease before antibiotics; he probably committed suicide in shame or remorse, or through insanity, as syphilitics suffer a lingering mental deterioration into madness).

Searching for the right whore, Dr. Stanley chanced upon others, all of whom may have been friends or acquaintances of Mary Kelly, since they all worked the same few blocks in the same loose-knit profession. (Consider the French Quarter prostitutes in present day New Orleans, for instance.) He got what information he could from them privately, and then strangled them. After this, he cut their throats to erase the marks of his hands. In a blood frenzy by then, he ripped up their bodies horribly, frustrated in his quest for the "murderer" of his son, as the weeks of fall, 1888, slipped by. Finally, on the 30th of September, he had her. But she turned out later to be Long Liz Stride, another whore who lived with a man named Kelly and who sometimes went by his last name. Mary, of course, is a name sometimes used by prostitutes, just as their customers are known as Johns, so the coincidence, the mistake, is understandable.

When Dr. Stanley did find Mary-Marie-Jane-Jeanette Kelly, he tore at her savagely in her room, taking his time, avenging the awful death of his beloved son. He then fled to South America, a common asylum then as in our era. This is the story told by Leonard Matters, an Australian reporter who claims to have come upon Dr. Stanley's "confessions" when Matters was an editor in Buenos Aires.

The only shred of Evidence for this enchanting scenario? The son of a man who worked in the City of London mortuary reports that his dad told him a Dr. Stanley (which Matters claimed was not the real name of the doctor) was a friend of the City Coroner, and often visited the mortuary. One day Dr. Stanley said, "The cows have got my son. I'll get even with them!"

Then the murders began, and after they stopped, the special visitor no longer came to the mortuary. The coroner said, "I believe he was Jack the Ripper." At least, so the son says the coroner, a Dr. Sanders, told his dad.

Kosmanski—Klosowski—Konovalov— Chapman—Pedachenko—Ostrog   THREE

Incredible as it may seem, it is impossible to sort out whether the above Ripper suspects are one man or several. Pedachenko was a mad Russian possibly written about by the maddest Russian of all—Rasputin. He was sent by the Russian secret police, long before the Communists took over, to undermine the English police force. After his business was done, he returned home to Russia, murdered and hacked up a woman, and died in a mental hospital in 1908. He might have worked as a barber-surgeon (it's all Cutting) as his London "cover," possibly under another name, Konovalov, who is mentioned in a Russian police bulletin as wanted for the murders of five women in London, one in Paris, and one in St. Petersburg (this document is lost.) Konovalov/Pedachenko, it has been established, knew several of the Ripper's victims.

Now Klosowski, a Pole with some medical training who was employed, it is known, in a hairdressing shop, was known to the police as George Chapman. He was arrested for poisoning three women, and was hanged in April, 1903. Ostrog was a Russian doctor and homicidal maniac (?) who could have been Pedachenko, who could have been Kosmanski (sometimes Kosminski), a Polish Jew who lived in the area of the murders and who hated women. He was confined to a lunatic asylum in 1889.

Chapman was definitely Klosowski (or Zagowski), which the English pronounced "Schloski." He was a womanizer, a bigamist, and possibly a trigamist, who liked to live with women two at a time. His wives looked great when the police exhumed their bodies—

arsenic actually works as an after-death preservative! This Bluebeardish domestic poisoner hardly seems the butchering sort, when all the evidence is in—and what use would Chapman have for whores, since women loved him? Exactly one use, you might say. If Pedachenko was Konovalov, aka Luiskovo, why not plain old Jack the Ripper as well? First, was he Chapman, and who's Ostrog? Apparently Abberline, in charge of the investigation of the Whitechapel murders, became convinced that Pedachenko and Chapman were the same man, and he should have known. Upon Chief Inspector Abberline's retirement, his team of seven detectives presented him with a fancy walking stick. This cane has a face carved on it, which looks as Russian as Rasputin's. The inscription of the cane, containing its history, reads in part: ". . . Abberline favoured the theory that the Ripper was a Dr. Alexander Pedachenko or Ostrog . . . and the head of the stick may well be based on his features."

James Kenneth Stephen   FOUR

Now we begin our approach to the most celebrated and illustrious of the Ripper suspects, who will be our sixth. James Kenneth Stephen, our fourth, was tutor to Edward (Eddy), the Duke of Clarence, during the two years this grandson of Queen Victoria studied at Cambridge (he seems to have been an indifferent student, if not actually stupid.) About two years after Clarence left, not much the wiser, Stephen had some sort of accident: according to his family's recollection, he was struck by a train; one writer claims he backed into a windmill while horse-riding. An unlikely accident, if there was one, if this is not another case of hushed-up syphilis causing brain degeneration, caused Stephen slowly to go mad. Stephen's father himself had a brain disease which forced his early retirement—within a year, the son died in an insane asylum, in February, 1892.

So Stephen was mentally "fit" for the job of Ripper. Did he have what might pass in the insane for a motive? Well, he may have, if he was homosexual, and if he fiddled about with his royal student at Cambridge, and if when Clarence left the bereaved Stephen, whether or not they'd consummated their affair physically, the tutor then came to revenge himself on the unreachable "Eddy" by knifing prostitutes.

For a wonder, we have concrete evidence which everyone accepts for at least part of the Stephen theory. He had an intensely sick hatred of women—his *poems* prove it! And his handwriting is close to that of a couple of the likelier genuine Ripper letters to the newspapers—again, the proof is in the poems, so here are excerpts.

I did not like her, and I should not mind
if she were done away with, killed, or ploughed.
If all the harm that women have done
Were put in a bundle and rolled into one,
 Earth could not hold it,
 The sky could not enfold it,
It could not be lighted nor warmed by the sun;
 Such masses of evil
 Would puzzle the devil
And keep him in fuel while Time's wheels run.

So Stephen hated women sufficiently to be the Ripper, and he was insane, and the handwriting is a good match. It's to be noted, though, that Peter Kürten's handwriting (he wrote letters to the German newspapers in conscious imitation of the Ripper) changed so much in times of stress that he could in complete security show these letters to his wife, who saw no resemblance and who never suspected her husband. Kürten was indicted for nine murders and revealed as the Düsseldorf Monster of the 1920s, and guillotined.

There's yet another piece of primary evidence pointing to Stephen: a very large piece. Dr. T. E. A. Stowell, using the private papers of Sir William Gull (he said), claimed an "S." was the murderer.

A last fact about Stephen: he was a cousin of a famous writer, giving a new twist to Edward Albee's phrase, "Who's afraid of Virginia Woolf?"

Lees and Gull   FIVE

The Physician Extraordinary to Queen Victoria, as well as Physician Ordinary, Sir William Gull had means, could well have had motive, and certainly had opportunity to commit the Ripper crimes. He was highly placed enough that there might have been a cover-up by authorities to prevent a scandal of Watergate proportions.

In 1871, he successfully treated the Prince of Wales for typhoid fever. Victoria made him Baronet and Physician Extraordinary for this; he was already Physician in Ordinary to the Prince of Wales and to the Royal Family in general. According to Dr. Stowell, Gull told Eddy's father, the Prince of Wales, that Eddy was dying of syphilis of the brain, called paresis.

Now, R. T. Lees, a spiritualist medium, used to hold séances for Queen Victoria. Once he saw the Ripper on a bus, but his wife and a hastily-summoned policeman wouldn't pursue the vehicle. In describing the Ripper from a clairvoyant vision, Lees said the killer wore a dark tweed suit and a light colored overcoat. He also "saw" mutilated ears in a vision—without knowing that the police had received a letter threatening to cut a victim's ears off. This caused the police to listen to Lees a wee bit more attentively. Together Lees and the police attempted to track the murderer; this search ended at a fashionable West End house belonging to a highly reputable physician who is unnamed. Was it Gull?

This doctor's wife told the police that the doctor was not at home when the murders occurred, and that he had "a sudden mania for inflicting pain"—once beating their cat, and at another time, their son.

Also according to Stowell, the doctor, when questioned, admitted to gaps in his memory, unaccountable bloodstains on his shirt, and facial scratches.

The clothing Lees had seen was found in the physician's closet.

Confronted with all this, the suspect wanted to commit suicide, but was instead placed in an asylum, where he eventually died. Was Gull thus secretly imprisoned, unknown to history?

Eddy, Duke of Clarence   SIX

The most important mystery of the whole Ripper case is the question, why wasn't Jack ever caught? Perhaps he was. If he was known to be the Queen's grandson, the heir to the Prince of Wales who became in 1901 King Edward VI, then certainly there would have been a cover-up. His Royal Highness "Eddy" could conceivably have been locked up by the Gov't in the form of the Prime Minister, Lord Salisbury; if not for syphilis, then for a "related" insanity, one of a violent sexual character. Again, Stowell, using what he said were the private papers of Sir William Gull, wrote an article accusing "S" of the crimes. Although Stowell denied pointing the finger at Eddy, and is now dead, much of what he wrote does indicate the Duke of Clarence was the Ripper.

Although Clarence has been alleged to be in Scotland, shooting game on the occasion of the first and second murders, it is well known that royal families have, throughout history, used doubles. Although it's irrational to expect other Ripper suspects to have had look-alikes used as stand-ins, that's not the case with Clarence. Anyway, it's entirely reasonable to suppose that the other Royal family members would have hushed up anything to protect the Crown, and that persons in Her Majesty's government would have spared no effort to protect the Queen. Clarence is a better match for the eye witness descriptions of Jack than anyone else, for Clarence wore the deerstalker cap as part of his familiar hunting costume. Stowell thinks that perhaps by "dressing" deer Eddy got a rough idea of how to dismantle the torsos of prostitutes. Was Gull, who was rumored to be seen in the Whitechapel neighborhood at the time of a murder or two, there to pick up Clarence, certify him insane, and "take care of him"? And perhaps with Netley the coachman's help, to finish off a lingering girl or two, or make it all seem the work of a horribly deranged madman, even if Clarence wasn't one, but was simply (!) a killer?

Stowell claimed Eddy didn't die of flu (a very serious illness) in 1892 (so goes the official bio), but of syphilis, also more serious then than now, in an asylum. Now Stowell's "S" was often seen in a male whorehouse in Cleveland Street which catered to aristocratic and wealthy homosexuals, and Clarence's personal equerry actually had to leave England to avoid a scandalous trial after he'd been nabbed in a police raid there. Perhaps Eddy killed because he'd contracted syphilis from someone, which made him periodically violently insane. Was "S" Syphilitic Clarence?

Prostitutes in London were frequently diseased. Although it has not been proven that Mary Kelly (or the others) did have syphilis, one must keep in mind the state of medicine over one hundred years ago, and it is a matter of fact that the coroner suppressed evidence at the inquest into Kelly's death. Eddy might have gotten it from Kelly, or from one of her friends; he might not have known for sure who was responsible.

According to a certain Sickert, Mary Kelly had been a witness to Eddy's marriage to a Catholic girl (unthinkable for British royalty), which had to be erased from the earth as though it had never happened: the mother institutionalized, the prostitutes (possibly because of attempts to blackmail Clarence) all killed, as if by a madman. The Duke of Clarence is, in many ways, most likely to have been closely associated with, or simply to have *been,* the man called by some "Jolly Jack." Why did the police relax after Mary Kelly's murder?

Had they truly caught the Ripper?

The Butcher

When I reached the ship in its bay, I upbraided each man for the guilty deed, but there was no amending it. The cattle were dead, and for another six days my comrades fed off the finest of these beasts of Helios which they had driven off. Yet the gods were not slow to manifest portents. The hides of the slain beasts crawled slowly along, and the meat (alike the raw and the cooking) bellowed with a lowing like the lowing of a herd.

—"The Oxen of the Sun" in Book XII of
The Odyssey, tr. T. E. Lawrence

The red plague rid you for learning me your language.

—Caliban

Kosminski, Schminski. Schloski. A meaterialist from an island,
shipwrecked. a cunnibal, a womandering Jew who (no Hun I)
bites cunt-guts. Antifaust I, Christkiller, kids said. Kinder lie.
"The indescribable.
Here it is done.
The Eternal Feminine
drags us down
and rakes us in."   And how may I help you, Mum?
(Blackness this utter emits white blinding
as the crushed light that forms the paste
inside sheepbones. The gash glue holds, it holds.)
Leg loin flank in a basket, who's my girl.
Breast shoulder shank in a casket I'm your man. Wholesale and
    retail cuts.
I am polish, you can Czech on that. Austrian, Estonian, nicht
what? I was born with a caul and had my true face, the onion skin
ripped from my underskin and peeled out of my spilling eyes,
torn out of my maw, screwed loose from nose sockets, unnailed
from the hammers in both ears. Ligaments, tendons, sutures.
    Unlike the
afterbirth potion, my caul
was saved, enwaxed and mounted, like Beethoven's
afterdeath snarl. I have both here in the back

of my shop. What woman's legs crossed my eyes? The sheeted
doctors lied, taped a pig's snout to my wound,
said one in ten million, taped and trimmed and cut
and wrapped my extra fingers and the webs. I woke to straitened
    sight.
        Have you heard the latest on Queen Vicky Vagina,
a Deutscher in love with the dead as I,
carries a piece of His ivoried brain in a pearled palm-bag,
prays to this Messe. *This is Albert's body and juices.*
Christ I'm famished. Marbled wealthy legs sieving grease
in the wiretopped fat kettle. Mr. Hare
or Mr. Hyde, or is it Burke you seek? Not Jekyll? There's no
gentleman here, just a heinie jew. Shhh. Even God whilom snacked
on his boulderish rough sons. Pardon my tongue, I almost bit
    while eating
on the wrong muscle, I mean my ham hocks, rinds, links, chops,
    gristle, bone.
Shards of the body's masonry, calculus it skeins in sunless bags,
a Cretan goat, firepit for roasting the plucky haunch
of the fisherman Homer's girlfriend
(her brain's mash *batter,* her liver *wurst,* he said).
I am but meat myself, hunks of bloodwashed hands squirming
with the knife that slips and plays. You must let the blood out
    through
the throat or it's not kosher. So I've heard. I'm not a hebe,
twelve kinds, tenderloins, steak and kidney, lamb's
jelly rolls. Every fifth entrant who tinkles
my little lead bell, by-the-by, puts a hand blindly
into the ice tub and withdraws a thing
he can take home or eat here, black forest cake
and grizzled mustard, many picks of meat pies, shepherd's delight,
pig and whistle, haggis candy, cook it, raw it,
eat anywhere but here in my shop. My secret sign hangs out,
the skinned dog, Das Hund, yet I am Moorish, I admit
nothing, so shoot me. Knife my children. Burn my alley cats alive,
I'll hold the women down for you too, when you're ready.

I am the flower of outback Tibet, the kingdom
of one, an exiled madman from his mind free, free
as Lazarus, stinking of grave hamburgers, liebestod pastry
of a life's time, tut-tut. Your lovely leech-lips suck. Try one of
    mine:
At the brain's base the mandrake root
cries
like a babe—in a Welsh woman this is shaped
like a bunny rabbit, like her pink lower ears,
folded as a limp bouquet that stinks.
               The door's ding tinks.
Let them not say I fail
to eat what I kill. This bit of tripe—raise
your gnawing hand if you know
of what balled cock consists—I'm not Russian you, huh?—
care for the latest, a "hot dog"? Rat turds, rattails, shards
and merds (what dead-city diggers term "coprolites"—Swift, my
    countryman,
was a Coprophagist, shit-eater to you and me.) Not so fast. A
    sample, free.
Intestines may contain traces of the last 30 or 40 meals you've
had, in many stages of de-compost. How many feet,
how many ells of your past life do you carry
with you in your midriff eels? Remember breakfast a month ago?
The gut's memory surpasses the brain's. So if you're nabbed
       use a finger inked in feces
       to scribe limericks about them
        on the wall of your last cell. (Are you not hurt? I nicked
        what?)
My long inner otter can squeak of my meals
and my women's meals, for I've tasted their
intestinal stew, and one had a few
small worms of her own—that's in Scripture,
ain't it—surely ye shall find
worms within worms? But I'm hungry
enough now to chomp a horse's dong, a fat long

one wrapped with kraut as sauer as
ladyfingers, which I'd have thought
to be sweet. They weren't. Have a nip on me, luv. CLOSED FOR LUNCH

Alphabet Potluck: Blackpoem

I crawled, swam, waded, ate my way past muck
Down one lane called the gullet, out the holes.
Where we are made is waste, love's filth to fuck.

What's brown or grey tastes best. Pink goes to black.
Till you've peeled the sun's scab, licked the moon's back
   holes
You haven't tasted best. Spit in the crack,

Spread globes, step in the dark that wrinkles slack.
The sideways eye birthed me too grave. Both holes
Are at my ends. Between the twinned are struck

Eyes, hands, tits, elbows, tongue halves duck and buck.
Up purgative's hill, down to hell, best of luck.

That red-lit chamber
where my heart's hand knocked on yours
and you opened, burst out waving
and ran flowingly to me, leaking the dead child
from your gut, that's where God's eyes watched.
From the heart's womb. Bleed her into health.
Give a pig stigmata wounds. Cup out that eye that slips
from front to back, appears on tits, sticks
out her phlegmish mouth. It was a sick man, east of Rio,
that first et oysters, tobaccy jism muscle
in a frozen cunt cone, granite thighed tooth sheath.
An oyster never, some say, dies, but lives through the worm
we call digesting's track. The disgusting trek
spews it down the human underground with its brown grey eyes
spat most full of horror's juice, blueblack pigtail squirts,
a tele-photograph of what we are, seen from inside,
snapped and stacked, condensed on itself to a dung-slug: oysters,
   shelled.
I once bit off a nipple, bricked her head,

then licking the blood put me off my food,
after I drank my gill, I mean. And broke her crown, half. Six bob a
    slice.
You want that wrapped, Father? Something for a holy
man, we call this the Pope's Relic, it's stuffed
with special mushrooms, imported. Morels, that's
them. And seasoned special. Trade secret, that,
the Holy Parts secreted in the Vatican, mummy-fied. Next, *wot*?
Not in the sausage frame of mind, then, Guv? (That gel's
one for the knacker's, mate. Ya see the cod, the fish
I mean?) This here's the sheep's eggs, balls they are
to you and me, but not the ladies. Sly as hogs at gates,
they tighten their butts, like to watch me sling
the blood and guts as much as blokes, tighten
their butts, sway out on the bell's kinkle-joinks.
Com'ere lad, feed your bird, tuppence a bag,
she's got two, it'll get her heat up same as you,
sure Spaniard flies they is (I raked em off a ham
that set too long and sprouted feelers. Maggots is blind,
you see, they grow spontaneous on dead meats, the escarguts
I slip into this tart's shepherd pie might have et
a great lord. Joy of the worm, all! A taste for long pig
what I'se crave since I et that nipple and pocket o' tit
and sucked it flat, I had to squeeze her other bag empty
and then I went on snackin and pickin at her, tastin
the fatty haunch, tight inner thigh pale as fish belly.)
You know what's good? News for yous, pal, you et it
yourself last week in that lot of stewed meat. (Knocks one? Enter.)
The sauciest girl, she was worms inside thick as
my middle fingers, but any intestine makes a casing
for blood sausage—who looks close? You grip yer nose
tight to eat it anyway, right? The grindstuff I call local
blender? Bubble and squeak you've et, and tripe on this slab,
such as haggis, now you've had the long pig's noodley
guts, and you're no worse off. It stinks like shit
of course, but tastes like nothing GOD rot.

"Stuck a finger in her gut
and called it macaroni!
Yankee butcher keeps it up."
(Here's one secret—I've sewn both of my thumbs
and the pointer back on three times—the last,
right down the grinder went them both off the good left hand!
These I've got on now aren't even mine—guess whose!) One
        moment.
Squid, chad, roe, sea cuke, octopus. One dried lung.
Kite string's used to tie off the bung, that's true. Flies, fly.
Take this fist of meat, drink this cup's piss.   Prick
with sharp fork often to allow grease to flee. "Cuckolds
are made with venison tripe." A worm to the wise.
You'll pay me later, Father, in the meatmarket down your way.
I keep me busy as a new bug.   CLOSED FOR LUNCH

THE RED LIFE: Doggerel on a Side of Beef

Whose hands lengthen her spinelet on my loom?
This razor excavates straight from the heart.
We fall into the stomach from the womb.

Red thrashers, fingers thrusting through vacuum.
A piece of poison apple corks the heart.
From caves we crawl to rise within our tomb.

I breathe inside your lungs and find no room.
I heave out innards deep within heart's heart.
I wrap me in your skin, cocoon of womb.

This backbone cross I wear with caul mushroom
Has bled a Niger in the swollen heart.
On threads of flesh we float to one kiln tomb.

Was there a maze beyond the hell of home?
I started carving when I lost all heart.
Meat art I make of women in this tomb.
Eat hearty, fill you every man his womb.

(The Guard wants changing. Horses fart black slime.
They pound me with a rib that pricks the heart,
till nights from mares to highest arch I climb,
from Big Ben tower at stroke of dawn, False Tart.)

How about a pickled Jew's Lip? I'm from York.
Carnival means to remove the flesh, some say. Read my signs,
    Mme. Ouspa,
in my ice-tubs of entrails. No icey block
is ever clear, like the floating eye at the thickened
bottom of your grog glass after six slugs, it stares as you stare
at the mirror hole, brown and blinkin like your own, makes you
    wonder
who's really watchin, mum? or da? and order another,
and watch the eye in the butt of the glass grow round.
Some intestines float in the impure ice, fog-guts
flow slowly in the frozen logs, marbled albino meat
with veins, rich ones of fat girls' ribboned hairs. Chew a rind or
    twist
of suet the longest day, I can, as I watch tendrils twist
into faces. Animals, mostly. Like sugar cane I had as a kid,
it keeps the teeth sharp, the faceballs wary.
Skating at night by tallow light across the waxed
floorboards, I walk my planks. My candles of lamb's fat
bleat greasy light in cold fleecy ringlets of air, thought's
scrap and thick chunk.   Once I et a hulk of whale,
called blubber, like a skin of foot-long jelly on the bloody
great beast, the leftover Thumb of GOD. It deity'd me. I wallowed
in a room I filled with more meat, a great many cuts of steaks, bears
shaved of their ladies' coats. I floated in blood and fucked
the holes I found in every organ, my swollen lump knifed wounds
it filled and hammered wider and left its wick's drippins in. Knot,
    wick.
I came a hundred times I swear and sold it
wrapped to gents and ladies, high and low,
to him and her and him and you. GOD bless your day.
There is fresh meat on the hoof in the offal alley,
I'm off to tripe avenue, trash land. I sharpen twenty
kinds of gleams, blades slit me many times, many yards
long they streak, they tattoo my long blood lines. Shall I kill
her with my knife or use my Bone? My marble eyes drip slow,

31

gelid. The many-penny nails in my mouth are now
open for business, guess what's on sale, don't ever slip, guess
what part of me I cheat with on the mirror-scale.
Meat artist, con-et-sewer—the piggies' eyes and noses I've
    thumbed
in loose bulk pork! Thin headcheese slices I shave that you
may view your own ghost through. See here?
My marble counters, hundred-weight scales, meat hooks I clang,
yes many are the riches a butcher has, his weighty lumpen worth.
Yet her hole was equal to the sum of my pants, its snakey girth.

(Closing time—here's Truth! I *did* one once had a
thing in her quim like a vise. It bit me off, down there, and now I
wear a boner that's perpetual, solid as a kidney stone. This member
has a sharpened tip to give the old gels something new, you get my
drift? They die for love of me, scratch scores of whores. Yet some-
thing's missing—when I cum, it's like I soiled m'self—it just leaks
down my britches like a handful of hot snot.)   Nicht *what*?

The Priest

This sacrifice, of what I most love,
    take it who will. One key
        for both Heaven and Hell.
They said I had a Calling and were right.
    I have heard voices. I hear them daily and at night
        now. Of course, those are the demons urging
me home to the Pit, but earlier, as a pale child
    when the others hissed at me and spit,
        for I called my clothes my vestments even then,
and saved my sweets for Whitechapel's whores' children,
    fourteen to a room with their "uncles" and "nephews,"
        relations together sinning in and on each and every body,
those we were taught were born damned.
    Better not to live . . . that's true, isn't it?
        What do you say, mistress mine, Annie Duckie, roving
hips, jack me off with your creamy tresses, the little pit
    at your knee's backside, the underswell behind, hmm,
        well, your behind? Some sermon this is, I realize, I'm lost,
always have been without a sound text. In this beginning, then,
    let your body be the Word.
        Amen, slut, the Queen of Heaven
had a body too, a round one like yours,
    a temple, a sun-caressed light-lave shrine. Lie still.
        White scar-slashes across your knees
where the reflex crouches, an imp with one trick.
    You must have fallen on them hard, not to pray,
        gashing them on pavement lips or on a glass razor's
tooth. You smile—those must be girlhood's bump
    and grind, when you ran fast as a late rabbit
        to escape, and afterwards wolfed as quickly down,
down the streets reversed to catch a cony-friend.
    (I'll return to that smile, a rotten come-you that yet works.)
        These flat feet mean you've donated as much as a constable does

of your tender soles, your inner arch. As you grew and grew,
   you walked the Chapel's maze, finding the center unchanged
      at midnight. You solved the journey many ways. You found
the Beast at the heart of this world. And now your belly tells
   the story of mute children who couldn't get out,
      who had to be born with a knife in hand. Your snub-nosed navel
(When is a woman small as a girl? When her knees touch her ears again.),
   stretchmarks like lice trails on the pelvis, all differing
      widths, indicate the gain and loss of the body's potato
weight, which is always the same, as you've found. It weighs
   precisely as much as the years, the number
      equals the latitude of breasts that once bulged hopeful.
(Angels on a pin's head, how many devils live under St. Prick's dome.)
   These nipples dangle cross-eyed at the end of brown loops,
      hanged. Your face lolls. Life is not written on the face,
the lies on the face are for others to view and believe,
   so I'll stop at the neck, snap its red garter
      belt, and go home. My confession is done. Is that not where I began?
Penance, shrift, absolution, fakes and marble tombs, cartoons
   on ceilings that will outlast God, perhaps. What is left
      that I believe?
Speak louder, use my mouth, I'll hear you, mouth-to-mouth.
   My breath you take, this quiet air
      tasting of sweetish dust, of death. Sweets do rot the teeth,
and out of the strong came rotten meat, that stink, Delilah.
   I've forgotten so much. I haven't preached in ages.
      When I met you I fell down six thousand years, down the snake's
mouth guarding the Garden. An Age
   of Reptiles, as some speculate,
      is the Beginning now, the beginning's changed. Why not?
What's rotten may yield medicine, as some plagues begin
   with a sweetened breath. Ring a round of rosy. I'm not listening,
      are you? This is always the hardest part, for me,
reclaiming Adam's rib, but it's a part of my symbolic Art.
   (The End justifies any Act. More later.)
      Why? So there will be one less damned priest and whore

in the world, and God is happier by having us in the place
    of torment. I'll do myself, but first I've got to mix
        your transformed blood in with the sacrificial wine,
so that the many may be damned as the loaves (a miracle!)
    were once changed into fishes. I mean the reeds
        became the slender boats of RA, the Pharaoh's staff, flowered,
ate the serpent petals of the Magi, no that's
    another fairy tale. Once, Annie, you told me you lived
        in a castle made of bad princes' bones and skulls as walls. Glass
and gold. A Beast with velvet tongue and coat fraught
    with vines served you an eternal meal. That velvet tongue
        I should remember, as I know I settled weekly
a wafer on its tip to watch you balance. What a trick
    you could do with it, juggling and flipping, elongating
        it like a red snake. We know what a red snake is like,
don't we now? My what a long beast it is, and your root
    is quite black. I'm afraid these teeth will have to go.
        Like plucking the petals of a wet daisy, girl,
(they're relics now, of you, mirror-saint, a nether-angel)
    he loves me now, she loves me
        not, god loves me now,
god love you, you've given so much,
    as I have. Hail a last time who changes blood
        into wine, this thin soup your squeezed cheeks
drip yields enough maroon nectar to soak full
    my white handkerchief. Last sacraments
        are so extreme, one drop will do, and the cross
made backward over your head, I think.
    I'll pray you'll intercede for me in the place
        where the damned are flames, and the veins
of the damned flow fire. I'm lying, my mouth sweats.
    Lust is raw meat
        that eats raw meat,
itself if no other feast
    is near enough in reach of its dripping jaws. Lechery
        is not a pale shade of Love as the Florentine wrote.

It is the Nth perversion, but do most great sinners
    believe as I, that their sin is the worst?
        That takes us back to Pride and betrayal. In Blood is Truth,
as Horace might have said. In sanguino veritas.
    A priest till death. Lost, I bear
        the sins of all the poor. I lay the living at death's
door, Lord even now your cunt leers at me
    with those wicked lips I love to kiss. To Hell
        with you. To Hell with me. To Hell with this,
with this. A man is a black gown, a woman is red death's masque.
    My secret, now, before you are cold—I want to be the First
        to be Bodily Translated.
(So few in Holy Writ were.)
    Not to Heaven, I don't believe in Heaven.
        But there's another list I think I can make,
if I kill every whore in London for His Honor's sake,
    to redeem . . . something given us, once. I'll never
        die, I'll be Taken Down, as Elisha who walked
with Him, was taken up. The Dark Lord has promised,
    will translate me to Hell without a death.
        There's a glory in that, I believe,
as who would not give all to see a Darkness Visible?
    I wish to burn in the fire that never refines,
        where the dead seas part. I desire to suffer
as long as God rules, as long as Sin lasts.
    Hell is close as the space between the heart's pumpings
        (when the rat that lives at the brain's base starts)
for any beat could be the last, and one someday must be.
    I talk and talk like any priest,
        and I forget you're dead. Our time is gone.
I'll pray for you, you sinner,
    you whore-flock. Someone's will
        be done. And at the hour of my death,
who can say? At the base of the brain,
    something
        starts.

The Poet

Jack and Jill went up the hill
to fetch a pail of blood.
Jack came down.

Horses clop-jop and the stones clap back.
    Dawn to dusk below my window, hansoms
traffic, coaches sway, the mailboys run.
    Any teacher might desire correction universal,
sempiternal. The errors I've inked on Latin
    examinations and failed speeches from the Bard
or Ossian—*When and I was a bonny prince With hey ho*
    the wind and the rain I kissed the girls and made them
wince . . . those lapses into vulgate japes,
    smeared blackly into a presentation copy
of the Odes. (Nota bene, Lector! Fugit, fugit.)
    I gave my pupil once, the special and only student
I now have in my charge, Baudelaire's translation
    of the mad American, Edgar Poe. *What I've done is*
six times since I've killed the whores and bled them
    dry. These sorties into sordid life
gave poor Clarence the headache for some days. He feigned
    to hear bells in men's speech, whenever more than three
gathered, after Poe planted them or rather burnt their ironwork
    into his lofty skull. His tiny royal ego like a bat's might flit
a'sway the buttresses, those arms of Titans sealed
    to the gorgon-rampant church. That ego would feel trapped
in gouged huge chambers of hulked air, stone-sealed up space
    such as the medievals sanctuaried in. I cast my gaze
as if on ropes to the street below, and distanced as I am
    from them, I fly high on sheer bone in my large wit's wind.
Jack Ripper was a man of blood
who delved in London town
John Ripping was a fiend of blood
who wore a scarlet frown

He bled the cows that chewed the cud
while walking up and down
He strolled about the East side streets
to catch a lass so bonny
the girl he chanced that night to meet
he'd call his darling Annie

The first drab that accosted Jack
had one eye blue and one eye black.
The second whore who tempted him,
her jaw could strike the divel dumb.
The third hag had but ane guid leg,
she leaned to leeward, pence to beg.
The fourth Jane called herself a Jill,
she might ha slithered up fra Hell.
The fifth one smoked a tar's black pipe,
she shanghaied him aboard her ship.
The sixth one had her own wee room,
she kissed and bedded all girls' doom.

The six are gone from London streets
they gave the wrongest man their best
Jack Ripper's left us, Hell to greet
and high class ladies in the west

Quiet. Time to dress and take a drab for midnight talk.
        One swift stroll expounding my finite terms, then I'll ask her
to solve an equation, something about what size of conduit
        can hold a bulk flow of one man's pent milk and honey!
I'll put her a case like Reverend Dodgson, the daft dean
        of Cambridge math: if a man runs all his life
in one spot, how deep will his grave plummet, compared
        to the chap Fogg who rounded the globe in
less than three months? I'll offer her a tanner,
        that Hamlet's gravedigger says will last for that
he's tanned in's trade. Like the stuffed ostrich Clarence

rode as a child, or did I only dream in a fever (how I've
suffered no man knows) Shakespeare played croquet
   with the black queen, flamingos flaming as night-torches,
queer beaks of cornucopia lambent the way certain faces
   do liquesce in small curd fogs? I'm burning up. I've got
to find a pupil quick and educate her my one Gradgrind
   fact, a construe from the language of woman to man:
what weighs on mortals heaviest, a pound of flesh
   or a pound of guilt on a sick man's brow, alight
enough to lead me through dark ways? Spare the rod
   and spoil the witch, that's in Shax too, or Francis, one
of the Bacon Brothers, the alchemist who changed base
   omelettes to hen's gold. Transmute this syllogism,
this serd won't bend, change me into a studentist again.

Pantaloon, by J.S., a Poet-at-Large

My little niece, your bubbles pink
   as baby fingers swell
my eyes. I'd more than wink
   at such, but soon all Hell
I'd catch. The Duke's thin spies

appear as if from books,
   to stalk the cornered bed
where we might meet. Gadzooks,
   what truth in fancy's head?
My beard, once brown as tea,

grey now, a weed, falls out.
   What thorns my baggy pants
have caught, what lies! Don't shout,
   my pet. Our covered dance
mounts, leaps love's filthy grot.

Hold still a bit. If One
   should come in now, say it's

a certain phrase you con
     of Greek . . . . Your Grace! (The fit's
on me.) I'll keep my place

in your gracious employ?
     My God. These girls, young sweet
red flowers . . . Please, a boy
     as my next charge, while fleet
away our Virgin's hours.

My name may never, God willing, be known
     to any of the public, yet the pussies, whores,
the dregs of lees of womankind, are wept on
     by ladies, by the Queen, by England. Anonymity
is worse than to fart one's verse in Dante, from my arse.
     The last girl had a backward glance she knew
the one thing any man wants Hey ho the wind will scream
     After each student fails the test and dies, I tell myself
there's more in heaven and earth to learn. But teaching
     is unrewarding on earth, I tell my wonder-wounded
hearers, failing every woman I've ever known
     with my midriff worm, lank as a maggot's corse.
Hey ho the rain won't come

O that I was a lit-tle
ti-ny boy

The Psychic

What I tell you three times is true.
                    —The Reverend Charles Dodgson

As I said to the Chief Inspector,
I have these Visions like automatic writing
given me by certain spirits. My ego flies
into a tree and folds its head under
a wing of white and sleeps
as an idea framed in a photograph. The blacks
are dark as India ink and the whites
are those of Irish linen or ectoplasm,
the mucus residue fragrant of the soul's breath.
I see things clear as if
the town were set into a snow-filled globe
and shaken up, and the flakes settled
like feathers about certain houses, an inn
perhaps, and a man in yellow leggings
and a broad plaid scarf about his face
stumbles into the cold blue air,
his spectacles' circles tangent-lined
by bar magnet eyebrows. Swiveling in the shook
compass of his sudden lurch outside, maybe
from an innkeeper's lack of proper genteel addresses
not agreeable to a man of iron will, he turns
northeast and south and points a sharp nose
red as a washerwoman's right fist. I See him
eat mouthfuls of cotton air that steam
from his breast and seem
then sucked in back when they came,
as though he fed off his own inner steam
and had a fire somewhere always stoked up that flamed,
yes! There, in his dagger eyes, the red!
(I am told by my Control or assistant
that entranced, I flail about and even once

relieved my bowels as if privily chambered.
I may foam about the mouth, or fondle certain
anatomical peculiarities on my person—you should
pay no mind, though at the end of my séance
with the spirit world I am naked, soiled,
relieved and bleeding from most orifices. Second Sight
exacts a toll, than which the sacrifice of a
priest of Yoga excels no whit.) A second time
   I cast myself into the medium's fit, epileptically
   convulsing, thrusting the Ark-ish veils, stoney,
   columnar as Samson's pillars, aside by main strength
   of my own Will. Now the fogs are gathered
   into a wall wide as a zone, as if the equator line
   had been girdled about the stomach of Earth
   by a Titan team, brethren to Atlas, who held
   the sky out of their way and let them pull
   the Oxen of the Sun that cinched the Belt of Darkness,
   this Black Wall. It is only a symbol, I say,
   an image of a line in me. Thus I change its suede hide
   into a leather whip, then snap the snake's back
   and lay its shuddering spine length alongside
   a drained ditch. We are in streets that quarter
   in crazed Cartesian fashion an un-mathematical
   section of London, a Barbary Coast. My wits lean as I perceive
   the yellow leggings approach a woman of the Eve.
   She engages his arm. They smoke and talk. He leads
   her, or is he led? into a small courtyard, a refuse
   area where he diddles her quickly, like
   a small dog. I am drawn toward the shadow
   beast they form that shudders on the high brick cul-de-sac.
   It turns into a horse that bites its own rear quarters,
   the stars spill from its mouth below human eyes. I am
   awake again. Third time pays for all. You weren't
   overly shocked? Good. We'll clean ourselves, and you
   gentlemen of the press and the official force
   may meet me here in my lodgings for a finale

effort one week from today. I feel sure
I'm on his track. I smell him in the room, can't you?
Rouge on my cheek from her pocky cheek, a ribbon
from her bonnet's back bow is here,
in my own throat. I draw it out like a snakeling;
take it with you, proof I am devout.

      Join hands gentlemen and ladies, for our last
      assault on that region bending our known space
      as a right triangle bends, its straight lines
      arching to curvatures when laid on a globe. Above
      the earth, far away, I rotate casting off essences
      like scarves, scarlet burning to yellow, white-hot.
      (That sky man, knife between his knees, glares
      one red eye. He, the Hunter, sees.)
      Do not let go your gloved hands, no matter how wildly
      we spin, or you may be left charred in your souls.
      I depart the spinning sun and levitate in the fakir's squat
      down, down the hundred million miles
      to pierce the clouds above besotted England. The gate
      is one man's yellow mind, and my *ka* has his key.
      Now he is entering his own house. You see the number,
      and where he hangs his greatcoat and that familiar
      muffling scarf in an entranceway closet.
      He turns to us, and we can see his face.
      My face, it is my father's face. It is a face
      from hell, out of my dreams, I don't know
      him. It, it. Ignore this weakness of my egoism,
      something in me is too alike the subject. Please
      note the Ripper's address as you saw it in my
      Vision, and go, go home.
      And if you catch him, go easy, if at all you can.
      Cut him down on the spot like a dog.

The Physician

In 1891, it was not a crime in England to take drugs.

—Rumbelow

Evil: this "philosophical problem" is a germ;
wash your hands properly and exterminate
the brute.   May a physician violate
his oath to save Life by killing
unfortunates? Better off dead, one hears so often,
in so-called mercy wards where humanity
has been stripped from the meat and bone. We break
a limb that it may heal the straighter.
          There is an evil plague on this city, and it wears
a woman's face. I've said it.
          Her appearance invited me to righteous anger, for vanity-
of-vanities is most ugly on flesh, that veil of pretties.
Merrick, called Elephant Man, instanced the opposite truth.
More grotesque than a fractured gargoyle weathered
by the worst that windy rain can do, then broken by lightning-bolts.
It wouldn't do to meet his shadow
on your cab-seat, leaning in, or face him of a sudden
in a lamp's ovoid frame of lemon light when the smokes
clear, the fog and soot-cloud called London air. Lime-light,
for actors like Merrick's woman friend, haloes her beauty;
of course, she can't resist the fairy tale coupling
of their names and forms. Green and yellow vapors, then,
like an ancient dragon's sulphurous steamy breath, a Worm
cinched around the Isle at Hadrian's Wall, squeezing,
biting its tail and swallowing, swallowing gulfs.   I remember
the machine I created long, long ago in a child's bad dream.
Often I couldn't breathe, as if the weight of London
Bridge spanned my chest, falling fell. I fished for air
until my nanny held a wet cloth to my mouth and nose,
at which Mother cried, "You'll strangle him!" The wet air
worked. I seem to recall I built with endless green

hoses and a horse-pushed system of pulleys and steam
bellows leading down to the fog-horn end of Thames,
the Great Fogging Device. It helped my early asthma, saved
my life.   One magic night
it filled my room with artificial humid air
so thick I could not see to read the damp books
blotted with mildew. I threw open windows and doors,
many scores of them. Through the house I ran, through
many houses and streets, revealing naked persons,
opening every portal hitherto latched. Then I rested,
breathing soundlessly, clear as a star in water while
the grey air entered and swelled and ate and ate
the silent city. On gold and green snake skin, no,
scales of grey like George's armor, dull and eyeless
it clicked, sliding and hissing softly as a mother's
forehead kiss. When I all-four floundered back
to my feathered bed, my house was empty. There was only
fog, no furnishings, nothing of form. I realized
I was the wrong lad, born invisible to others,
too unhealthy for the sun to dry. Each house I searched
was different, empty. A river of dead clouds flowed
on the cobbles, masking the foundered horses, blind.
Then everything but the cloudbank was gone. I breathed
easily a smell of familiar decay, and I woke (I think
in sleep) to frogs rotting in soiled linen
I had thought to hide behind the bed. Asthma may be caused
by a wounded conscience, I've heard. Sin is the longing
to do what sane men dread.

                      A man alone in heaving fog
might stroll a ship's length a thousand leagues from land.
Like the Flying Dutchman, he'd clutch any hand,
even a pocked street drab's. I am a diver without
the weighted helmet, I bare my opened head. I can almost chew
the milky spun tufts, wrapped filaments of velvet stuffing.
Drink deep, someone says, swallow the long grey snake.
Take this, now. Work that pump. Open wide, sir or ma'am.

Like shoving a tube down a dead whore's throat. What
made me say it?

                    Surgeon of the City of London
                    policy force, Dr. Brown:
                    The throat was cut across
                    to the extent of about six
                    inches or seven inches. The
                    sterno cleido mastoid muscle
                    was divided; the crisoid cartilage
                    below the vocal words was severed
                    in the middle. Vocal *cords*.

Adult, a medical degree, I advanced highly, first tried inhaling
the stuff at school. Such journeys, to lands some say might be real,
somewhere in William Morris, at the Wood Beyond the Fog's
    Edge. Elevated
to treat the Royal Family, guard the Crown Jewels's keepers, sort of.
Administered ether myself to Her Majesty Empress of India,
the Queen. Victoria vomited and voided afterward, like
pea soup, the proverbial thick-mess of our sickening fogs. Now I'm
taking it again, the magic drug, of late. Ether, opium, befogged.
            I have such dreams, I can't tell anyone.
I walk in the early clouds I lowered onto earth
at my begetting. Black cables snake, green liquid runs.

They danced as if the fog were water,
steps of waves, knee-high and higher,
made plunging sounds with hooshing lips,
walked ever deeper into the sea-surge.
Hip-high and above, kicking and circling
him, keeping him (is it me) in their center,
bending closer, lower down. He smelled sea weeds,
the wet claws had him, their heads
lowered, bowed to bend upon him,
no more breathed he after that. He woke
among the sheets soaked with a salt-spray
odor in his large bed, his coverlet ripped
and chewed on which someone or something
had lightly bled.

I had to dream in the fog
again and more, even if the daylight city itself
went under to an eternal rest. In the sun-dead west.
The black pipes aided my flight, my windows closed, eyes
taped tight. I realized Stonehenge is the crown of a giant
God, four gods, concentric coronets. My bed
lay at the foot of the altar stone. Someone
said, Tag, you're It, and through lagoons
inside flooded castles and iron estates
a high voice ran. The black basalt altar
grew too large for the room, and drank
new size from the Thames, ate every drop
of water and the world shrank
and I woke. Every time I come home
from the grey lands, weeks have elapsed
and the new papers tell of new horrors.
Someone is doing murder underneath the yellow
lights of day. Someone is hiding. I go.

You're It, and you are counting
to a hundred backward, loudly
so all the house's dark corners
can hear. As you reach lower numbers,
you skip, often as you can, without
anyone hearing you cheating, uncover
your eyes, and move, eyes wide,
fingers alive, through the many paths
open to you. Under the sink
you pull the first one out
by the hair, snap its neck
quickly and move on. Under the bed
your sister is waiting. She is always
there. It is always fun when her blue eyes,
now black, jerk up, her lips open and close,
just once.   Now you are crawling, and upstairs
your parents' room is the only place left. Go
straight to the big closet and open both doors.

There they are. Where they always will be. Your dad's
breath is a wisp of a thing like a beard, and your mother's
brown eyes are so sad. You reach for them both at once, move
in close, and squeeze, like you'd squeeze the life out.
                    A woman emerges from the fog,
giving birth from her navel. The Physician, a pasteboard Healer
with a long goldish rod, offers help. She says she is not ill
and hands him a crybaby, her dead girl, then another,
then another, then another, then another,
then another. The seven link arms with him at their focus.
There is to be a sacrifice. Let me out of here. Obsidian
knife, bone handle incised with red odd-angled designs.
A white cloth the size of your head if the skin
was flayed and stretched like canvas. A clay pipe,
very old, squat, phallic. See tooth-marks. He was digging
in the barrow mound, hands eating the shallow rise,
unveiling a breast-shaped tomb four feet around. He broke
it at the torn or bitten nipple, pot-size, and found
it hollow. Its smashed sound felt like a stone sky
falling, a grey dome of stars in handfuls diving
into the pit. He fell and followed the fragments
of bone and baked mud, stone and coprolite, shards
and millenium-aged shit bricks.
    Voices around him, not me, through the earth
filthy with chunks of clotted sky. Brittle sounds
of water, hands slapping, clicking, rubbing, snapping.
Before language there was gesture. She raised a stone
scalpel, knife-edged, and lifted his organs out
                    All the injuries were caused
                    by some very sharp instrument
                    like a knife, and pointed.
and she read his future and he knew it was true, and he was dead.
He woke in fog and never left it, after these events
recorded in a journal bound in skins.
                    The cause of death was haemorrhage
                    from the left common carotid
                    artery. The death was immediate.

48

Light, a cotton wrap,
blurred her bare white knees.
     Death was immediate.

The Prince

(In a Madhouse Cell, "confined for TB," where he died in 1892)
Is there a murderer here? No. Yes, I am.
                                        —Richard the Third, a'dream

Her smell! First so enticing. When I raised
her underskirt a fistful of fly-dirt,
a clump like a wasp's nest clung to my hand,
buzzing, alive. Only a waking dream, but she truly
did smell of offal in a strong sun that held
its place like Jericho's until the Miracle
was completed: the stench of Hell's nether parts
belched forth on Earth. The gelatin surface
of even the sides of her head when I'd finished,
so that I constantly perforce wiped my hands,
even gloved, as they were, in fine kid. I am insane,
but I know so much: any woman's death diminishes me, for
I am involved in manking. In making. In kingdom-
keeping in this keep or castle strongroom. Ho,
a rescue! Another dragon brings me roast meat,
but I know that trick. I know what kind of rump
they'd have me smack my chops on. I'll eat my thumb.
Fee fie foes come. In the light pond birds she sat.
        In the lake-fed weeds, I mean,
        she sits. Wind
        rustles the stalks
        of her brown long hair.
        She spies me turning
        from the path, scatters
        drops of flashing
        water amid the rushes
        as she rushes
        and the light pond birds
        rise up, startled
        and everything flies at once.

A man who would be king, as I will
when the bloody work is done, enacts
from youth the fairy tale premise:
what to do to wake a sleeping princess;
how to stimulate those who feel nothing,
nothing; glass princesses who must be put
to sleep and those on ice-beds like served delicacies
for me to eat, fat and lean. My father is the man
who will be king, and then I shall be the Prince
of Wales instead of Duke of Clarence, an evil man
from Shakespeare's *Richard the Third*. Evil because
he let his brother imprison him like the blackbirds
in a pie. I mean the prisoner of the Tower who dreamed.
I too dream. I dream of waking me from these fairy tales.

That old cow his mother
wants Jack to sell
he swaps for semen drops
of power beyond that of mortal
fairy tale Englishmen. Why
won't she understand (there's
a *good boy* Jack) you stupid
lout she says and scatters
his magic first seeds
out the window. *Now*
someone's got to pay, to die
he says that night in sleep.
    Morning has grown a new root
in the brain. It's not something to tell
your mum, how you grapple
this deep strain and sweat
your way up the giant's overgrown
shaft to find the big man's
castle. He's home in his den, eating
chips from a bag of foreskins, chewing
hard on something bad in his guts.

He's a gone one, right then,
like the noisy rosy hen,
laying eggs, reciting Cluck!
and other words that end
with uck! Jack's the head bean
now, roll over, dad, your bag's
empty. Jack B. Nimble twitches an eye
and gives the loot,
of course, to Mum.
She strokes his rough-haired arm
with a fading charm
all night and every night
until gold dawn.

I acted the part of Good brother Clarence
in *Dick 3 Eyes* one Eton term. I do act and read in my prisoned days,
and re-enact. "Once more into the bitch, dear friend,
or close her holes up with an Irish, dead." Daily I answer the
    Goddess'
messages in dark Guiness bottles, in my new blue uniform, a naval
    Lord,
shipless. How do blackberries stuff two score of crows' feet
corpsed in the crust? In mental chains I heartily endure
for now, not once but future king of England,
and who knows, after that? I could rule any museum
of this world, my specialty broken tall clocks
and the painting of women screaming at the artiste.
A *Punch* drawing of a rouged woman near her time
of delivery resembles Oscar Wilde. That picture
of Dorian Gray resembles smooth Lucifer bad novels
call Vlad Dracula. I walk and guard
the basalt halls, stalking the eyes, resurrecting
each wrist turn the hand took, the crazed hook
of a glass elbow, how he stood back from a canvas
with Lord Douglas, Wilde's "friend," and admired
the naked men. Pregnant Oscar will have another boy,

I quipped. Fuseli framed my nightmare, more—
I step back and back, behind the Byzantine frame of the frame
and I am the painter, the painters, and every bizarre guard
watches me watching them. We came through a mirror called
Versailles, the Tate Gallery, and now
we exit through our mums and das
the Prado, the Louvre. Indolent man wishes to become
a right cast-off masterpiece by the Vinci bastard,
or have his mists illumined by Turner, ship's master,
like Victoria's fog-horn voice when she rolls
back the mists and births: Grandson, Let there be Night!
Your gassy delusions smell of grandeur. So mine, great Mother.
I want to add one syllable of true wine
to the cups of thin blood in veins so rich a vampire
might only sip and grow faint. A scene intervenes—how Dreams dig
a baker's half-dozen of cracked ladies up,
a field of tongues wag as if flowers might wing by,
tipping them pollen. Here is my Peace—one canvas in a cave of
    light-wet
stones I'd give the White Tower's jewels
to have here in my donjon, this cavehouse where
they shut me up for syphilitic brainrot. Stone-wrapped Virgin
of the light-tongued rocks, halos serving her and Anne
for crowns, and his thorn coronet outlined
in dotty chalk, the baby God. Is anyone reading
my thumb prints in the uneaten fare, these hints
I push out through bars to the bleak birds, father-
Fate's ravens, cindered doves, thrushes barking—
beaks whetted on the dead girls' eyes?
I take the air, a chain of bubbles sinking (broke's the crown)
down to the treasure chart, a rusty torso
shrimpeyed, snailnippled, the large fishes' eyes
seem nipple-centered, intestines pickled eels
jell hardboiled jarring eggs the balls. Pub comestibles
lined up on a sideways grandad timepiece, its slit a pinklit
crack, so a grandmother clock rather, appears suddenly

in my drear cell. Gargantuan. When they stuck me here
and blinded me for being Jack and not stopping It, I never
thought my eyes could grow back, but they have. I see under
the world. Each year has a dwarf shape and numbers tune
themselves inside my hands. I hear my brains beat, eggy
whisper and scream. I let me out:

        A dog came to sniff at her. I don't know
whose. One of the pack, part wild, that fades
    in, out of the plankings that form their enclosures,
gates being unpatched gapings in slum fences.
It was tawny-pied, long. Phlegm hung in a loose string
          from its tallow face. It seemed hungry, snuffling
    waxy snot on the poor woman's opened neck. In respects
more rat-like than canine (of the sable Rattus Rattus), the skeletal
      cur was jar-bellied though its bloated ribs could be
        numbered
with my thumb. I kicked it and felt a hard brace snap. Mine.
    The hound slipped off into some muck, heaps of trash
that bloomed about us, festering. Some smoke oozed along
        the foggy ground, spontaneous outbreath of the decay
        impatient to eat this city, these scum. Effluvium
of my spent desire. Rid by flame these sordid blocks
    of shame, a wasted people's dirty home. I saw pregnant
children, four years old! and thought
    what horror has so undone Nature
    as to surpass both Moral Law and Biology's claims?
        And still their bellies, empty, swelled. My personal
        physician
explained this as results of malnutrition,
    the bursting stomach and fish-big eyes were disease's
symptoms. The dog or half-rat had minded me
        of these children born in rot and soon to be fed
    upon in the brown heaps of rags and scraps. They
disgusted me.

I dream of a candle burning in my right lung.

My cell is warm. I am returned.
I open the clock to adjust its faulty face, for the time
is double-jointed and a girl in two pieces of some circus
cloth groans inside the cabinet's bulk. Each half of her
has tried to grow again, the usual trick. Leg stubs
and a tiny head, one horizon an anvil, the inland sea
a swamp of memories. A mermaid, but which half fish?
I dream the horror drowning in fog, then swimming
burnt by gas lamps featuring fish ornaments, seared
by the rushing horses' nostrils and mouth bits,
and the wreck is in my cell, my walls. This castle
is a'crumble, going, Oh God!
   Confession of a Demolished Castle
    All the dead horsies
     flew away through my wall.
     There isn't a full moon,
      or any stars at all.
    The night men come stalking
     by where the hedges grew.
     I hear their footsteps, walking.
     I see their shades accrue.
   Up in the darkling Tower
  I cry across the hills.
 I dream about my horses,
dead.

   I ring and ring the bells.

Going Down.   The above is not in code. No one censors my
 dreams.
Rescue your king. I've only
had a nightmare. Eddy's cold.

I am a curator or cook, a harmless knave of hearts, a Swiss
policeman, someone's cousin, anyone's husband.

Did I tell you I've had sixty wives? Eddy can like Caesar
be a woman to men, a man to women. But I've got to get
out and find those girls and clean their faces, set
the clocks right, and paint them alive. Your Sovereign,

Butcher, Priest, Poet,
Psychic, Physician, me.

O I am young and dead GrandMother
Vicky vicky vikky vikky vik.
I'm dead as Albert-Albion Grand-morte.
Vikky vikky
vicky vicky vic.
Visit me again,
the doors are wide.
            But
have I pleased you, Grand-damned?
Are you not "amused"?

A Memoir of the Man
Who Caught the Ripper

I dreamed that title every night for years
as the awful Eighties lapsed into the numbness,
the Nineties. Now I wake and count
threescore-and-ten. Last night in sleep
I wrote my report again—
> Using the method suggested by a crank
> letter to the *Times,* Chief Inspector, I hid
> dressed like a streetwalker in cul-de-sacs in Whitechapel
> until a gentleman came to pay. He desired
> to take me from behind, the stand-up way. It was He,
> and he struck, his blade ripping my ear
> as I triggered the neck mechanism (adapted from
> a Lady's corset) sent in by An Ingenious Reader
> of the newspaper. The Ripper's limb was pinched safe,
> the fiend's arm imprisoned and nearly torn
> clean off, like the monster's
> in that story. You say Her Gracious Majesty
> will personally reward . . . ?

Why after so long such a dream, why do I return
to those murders, as if he were the only one
who got away? Most such crimes go unsolved (although not I
nor any copper would let on to the public ear).
How many poisoners must there be, getting shy
of just the wife or monied aunt or hubbie dear,
poisoning the tea (tedious, obvious) of that one victim
and never repeating the crime? A century before
I joined up, servant women murdered whole households,
one by one, before they got an arsenic test. We'll never
know how many slaughtered families came down
with that personal plague, the disgruntled maid.
The poisoners then lived like me, and presumably Jack,
to a black over-ripened old age. Age.

Is that why I dreamed? It's the Biblical figure,
from the O.T., connected in the rubbish bin
of my mind with that quote the Ripper said
about Jews. On a brick wall,
in the madman's own hand—

 The Juwes are not the men
  that will be blamed for nothing
(a multiplied negative, like the Bard's
 Never never never never never.
Well what else have I done but read
since I came, say escaped, to New York.)
Was Jack the Shakespearian sort?
So I dreamed him because I'm seventy today.
It's a birthday gift from me to me
of what I left behind. I never solved those lines'
ambiguity either—

 Should the Jews (Joos? Juwes?) be blamed?
 Will *others* be blamed for nothing (in error)? Who?
Perhaps that spelling is the illiteracy
of the leather-aproned butcher we arrested,
daft mistake, a Pole who used his knife in's trade
and like ten thousand others,
wore daily stains of blood?
Or—

 the Jews are taking their revenge.
God knows, whether their God, or ours,
the dead one, the yids have had enough from
England. How many killed
of their Waiting kind? Enough to inspire
our writers forever: Shagspere, that's right,
Kyd and Marlowe and
 where's the *Tales*?
  the boy, a lovely Christian, killed by dev'lish Jesu-slayers,
  who walked the Quarter and sang a blessed hymn
  with his throat slit open,
  his tongue protruding, piping pure.

So Chaucer said, in his Book of women and men.
        Is that a help, a clue, was Jack a Jew
who did for Christians? Or was he another point
of the crooked star, a sot who is sure
he's Christ himself?
        No new theory here. It's long been dredged—
        the Ripper as Jill (say your nursery rhythms),
        a gang of bleak revengers,
        Prince Edward of the Queen's own descent,
        an American. A gorilla. Tsarist Russian. Ruddy
            Scot. The list of mankind.
I may as well
get back to bed.
This birthday's done. No Jewish solution.
No memoir from me as legacy
that anyone would ever read. Yet
one more mystery—why Himself, the Police
Commissioner, Sir Charles Warren, erased those lines
Jack chalked about Juwes in the dead
and dying night. He said he'd done it
to forestall public rioting, for the area is dense
with unrest, three households or families sleeping
in one room so cornered. They'll blame any stray goat.
But we'd the place, the whole "crime scene"
(new term for the old, old Eden thing)
well roped away from prying fingers and eyes.
There was no need to rub it out on that account.
There was scant cause to sponge those words, unless—   to save
Prince Eddy of the Royal House? Or Sir Charles
himself, gone suddenly off it, like more than one
copper, (or doctor, for that)—
        so crazed by the lunatic moon he'd gut a woman
        from her breast to her privates and continue
        on back, or stab her thirty-nine times, lashes
        of a white knife, so that her skin flapped
        like the tatters of a ravelled quilt, or quick

slice off those fat glands and lay
them staring on her eyeballs,
or the worst one, the last . . .

He had one finally in a room.
The youngest whore, so almost pretty.
(Only legend thinks those drunk bitches
appealing. God save their souls.) He'd got her closed-up,
the only one not done right on the paving,
and he'd worked all night sculpting Woman
into something less than stone, undoing
Pygmalion's mistake. All night, with a fire
nearby, to burn some things.

No inch of the flat hid from us,
each had its clue of blood, its pale handprint,
ruddy blots, splotches and organ-sneezed stars
of blood, pools, rivers, incarnadine oceans,
its threads from garments, over- and under-things,
its traces of him
and her. What was her name? To hide from us,
their "bloody peelers," they too used aliases,
as we did in plain street guise . . . and he?

one

redlips opening wider than
her head, the jaw
dropping in the throat's mess, the knife
dancing with his hand, eyes
giving the beat

two

a woman is a hole, two holes,
three holes. a woman and
a knife are thirty-nine,
which is all the holes

in the body of the world,
or in the world of her body

three

five children and no husband
and no money but body, and lots
of blood, and gin is cheap as Hogarth
etchings someone showed you, but gin is hard
to earn, to earn on your back, you've no smile
left, but this dapper gent
will make your throat giggle

four

a pair of streetstrutters so much
alike, they never knew,
wouldn't have cared
which went first to her body's
death. then around the corner
the other waited, hardly raising
her old eyes. it was only another
man, was her last thought

five

how wrong they were. he
could hardly remember being
just a man, always alone
and boy-lonely before the Other
came to live in his tight
hand and in his right arm
and chest, and in his lower
body. he pulled the Other one
on like a shadow. it fit

six

no one would ever see what
the last one's eyeballs did,
but didn't record. that film
over, went black, there was no sound
and now no need to go further.
it was done and none would ever know
and understand why he had *had*
to do them all, and why *that* way,
and why them, and why why him.
no one

Those words might *say* him, put his question
to rest. Or other words, chiseling or lacing
filigree in flesh.   The murders stopped.
The murders stopped. I worked for years
on other jobs. Sometimes a man (it's all down
in the *Times*) killed a string of fellow men,
or women, even, after that,
but it wasn't like Jack, whose fresh escapade
outdid the previous in awe and impossibility
of escape. There was only one true Ripper,
a methodless cutter who simply hacked with precision,
as if by habit ingrained, more shockingly
each time out. *One* bloke wrote those letters
(at least the one we know was true), enclosing
a kidney bit to the slum neighbors
who feared and formed the Whitechapel
Vigilance Committee—
        Dear Mr Lusk
                        I fried the other part and ate it
                            Yrs from Hell
                                    bloody Jack

The kidney matched
one left in Cathy.

I had eaten such organs
but not since then.
No, not since that. Nor have I married,
and I've had little since of sin—so many of us
of the Yard then never married, and I've always
taken heavily my mission. The chief said
    Men, it's worth your lives
    to get this one. All London shies
    from the streets. The city's dead. The Queen
    herself has got ideas for catching him . . .
    she sent a list, bless her, and last year
    marked her fifty-year Jubilee.
I tried. We all tried. Then it stopped,
and at the Queen's death in nought-one
I retired early as so many did.
And most of us have died.
    If there is a clue, will the future
find it, will *some*one, will you know?
And what would he do with such unnecessary
knowledge a century hence, the players gone
to worms? Write a book?
    And I cannot even now find sleep.
We called him Jack, who may have been any number
of killers, as you would call
anyone whose name's unknown. And the lot of us, folks
took to calling Bobbies and Peelers, after Robbie Peel
who formed the Force. (Bobbies when
they were got used ter; Peelers
before anyone would stand the sight of 'em
nosing in honest folks' affairs.)
We together were faceless as he was alone. I'm sure he was
one, alone—   Bob versus Jack.
Bob talked, and more than once, together
with himself, sum of the Law,
of what we'd do,
I'd do, when

we caught him. That word, that
"when." When-ness is all. Our all was nought.
My I was nothing. Jack's eye wins, one ayed.
          Last night I dreamed
about that too. We raged
like butchers, rock-sober, glass-shaven, jaws
forthright, so bloody right. The righteous Bobs,
each who has a bit of the jack (that's loot)
in his own skin.   For decades I've killed
the Jack army, weighing my heart in one flat hand, hearing
it flop. I was the army that chased me pursuing
single me. Enough
dreams. Any god keep me
from screaming.   I'm awake, now let me stay
awake and end the chase
right now.
And if I die
before I sleep—stop asking Why—
I Will.

Afterjacks

A qui veux-tu que je raconte mes cauchemars privés, sinon à toi?
—*En attendant Godot*

What terrified me, will terrify others. —Mary Shelley

Cum mortuis in lingua mortua (con lamento).
—Mussorgsky, *Pictures at an Exhibition*

Jack be nimble, Jack be quick.
Do you in with a candlestick. —children at play

Children frequently base associations upon a similarity of
movement which is overlooked or neglected by adults.
—Sigmund Freud

I am not a slut, though I thank the gods I am foul.—*As You Like It*

If I were God, I'd forgive everyone.
—Grushenka, *The Brothers Karamazov*

To God there is no zero. I still exist. —the Incredible Shrinking Man

Ich bin der Geist der stets verneint. —Goethe's *Faust*

In the Unconscious, as we are aware, No does not exist, and there
is no distinction between contraries. Negation is only introduced
by the process of repressing.
—"The Case of the Wolf-Man," S. Freud

I speak well, do I not, for a man in my situation?
—*Watt,* Samuel Beckett

Evil and brief hath been my pilgrimage. —R. Browning

Why wert thou not a creature wanting soul?
>
> —*Doctor Faustus,* Marlowe

Just you wait a little while,
The nasty man in black will come.
And with his little chop-per,
He will chop you up!
>
> —counting game beginning Fritz Lang's *M,* a film
> about the Düsseldorf Ripper, Peter Kürten

Faeces, baby, and penis thus form a unity, an unconscious concept
. . . of a little one that can become separated from one's body.
>
> —Freud

Is it okay to see them naked if you cut them up afterwards?
>
> —John Merrick in Bernard Pomerance's THE ELEPHANT MAN

Mother of Satan

Old Mother Hubbard
Sitting near the cuppard [*sic*]
with a hand grenade
under the oatmeal.

Who will you kill now
Daughter of Satan?

In the image of the
Virgin Mary—pure and innocent
The Great Impersonator—

Is that you? "Yes."
How many have you decieved— [*sic*]
lured to slaughter like a
fat cow?
>
> —A poem by David Berkowitz, September 22nd, 1976,
> a month after his first murder—*Confessions of
> Son of Sam,* David Abrahamsen, M.D.

Perhaps it takes a madman to see into the heart of tragedy . . .
—Northrop Frye on *King Lear*

In 1871, a Frenchman named Eusebius Pieydagnelle became obsessed by the smell of blood in the butcher's shop where he worked, and committed six murders with a knife, mostly of young women; he admitted that the murders were always accompanied by orgasm.
—Colin Wilson, *Clues: A History of Forensic Detection*

Well may the world cherish his renown; for it has been purchased, not by deeds of violence and blood, but by the diligent dispensation of pleasure. Well may posterity be grateful to his memory; for he has left it an inheritance, not of empty names and sounding actions, but whole treasures of wisdom, bright gems of thought, and golden veins of language.
—In Poet's Corner, from "Westminster Abbey"
by Washington Irving

But soft! Here come my executioners.   —*Richard III*

The James Dickey Contemporary Poetry Series
Edited by Richard Howard

Error and Angels
Maureen Bloomfield

Ripper!
Carl Jay Buchanan

Portrait in a Spoon
James Cummins

The Land of Milk and Honey
Sarah Getty

All Clear
Robert Hahn

A Taxi to the Flame
Vickie Karp

Growing Back
Rika Lesser

Lilac Cigarette in a Wish Cathedral
Robin Magowan

Traveling in Notions: The Stories of Gordon Penn
Michael J. Rosen

United Artists
S. X. Rosenstock

The Threshold of the New
Henry Sloss

Green
Sidney Wade